HOW TO TUNE YOUR VIBRATIONS TO THE DIVINE

DORIAN GREER

SPIRITUAL VECTORS

Copyright © 2021 by Dorian Greer

All rights reserved.

No part of this book may be reproduced in any form or by any electronic or mechanical means, including information storage and retrieval systems, without written permission from the author, except for the use of brief quotations in a book review.

To My Guardian Angel

I wouldn't know her again if I saw her. I wouldn't recognize her voice.

Getting through the TSA checkpoint, I had to reassemble my belongings. I was putting my shoes back on, crouched over a semi crowded row of chairs. I was leaving Arizona on a flight to Detroit.

I had a hundred things on my mind. I hate crowds. I'm somewhat introverted. I was almost done and good to go.

Out of the blue, a young woman walks by me and says, "I believe this is yours," and hands me my wallet. I had left it behind in a dish. It wasn't a TSA agent, either. Just a regular, good, person who decided to save a bumbling idiot from certain disaster.

I thanked her as she kept waking. I wouldn't know her again if I saw her. I wouldn't recognize her voice. But her act of kindness will forever be remembered as long as I live.

My wife says I have a guardian angel. I don't know. I'm pretty sure she was human.

"Thank you" kind person. I don't know if you're a guardian. But I do know that you're an Angel. "Thank you!"

My name is Dorian.

THE NEXT GREAT LEAP OF HUMAN EVOLUTION

We are fast approaching the threshold of advanced knowledge. Our civility has not kept pace. The failsafe, our own destruction, has an override key. It is the evolution of consciousness.

Start here.

— DORIAN GREER

CONTENTS

1. THE SPIRITUAL ECOLOGY — 1
   The Spiritual Ecology — 1
   What Isn't a Spiritual Person? — 3
   What Is a Spiritual Person? — 5
   Tuning Your Vibrations in The Physical World — 7

2. THE SOUND CURRENT — 13
   The Sound Current — 13
   The Efficacy of The Sound Current — 16
   How To Ride The Sound Current — 18

3. THE VIBRATIONS OF DIVINITY — 23
   Sounds of The Divine - Spoken — 23
   Healing Harmonies from The Universe — 26
   Which Vibrations Matter? — 28
   Consciousness Altering Vibrations — 29

4. TUNING YOUR VIBRATIONS — 35
   Vibrations: The Light & The Sound — 35
   The Conduit of The Spiritual Body — 37
   The Pitch of Your Vibration — 40

5. HOW TO JOURNEY INTO THE SPIRITUAL REALMS — 51
   The Techniques — 51
   The Spiritual Currency — 57
   The Spiritual Challenge — 60

6. MUSIC FOR INNER TRAVEL — 71
7. BACK MATTER & REFERENCES — 77

1

THE SPIRITUAL ECOLOGY

THE SPIRITUAL ECOLOGY

*T*uning your vibrations to the divine is an essential act of spiritual alignment.

To you, it awards the greatest treasures the divine can offer. To the world, it awards the greatest treasures that *you* can offer.

In the material world, it unfolds from the cause-effect consequences of *actions*. Those actions advance like a Rube Goldberg machine to its inevitable conclusion in every direction. Even when there is no one left to remember you, the effect you had on the universe remains.

In the spiritual worlds, however, it operates purely from the depths of *awareness*. This is how it unlocks the gates to higher realms and reveals your nimbus - the *design* of your consciousness as a discernible emanation.

It is the pattern of your consciousness as it resonates between the external world it perceives, and the internal world of its interpretation. It's a visual of the conduit. It's fascinating; I'll show you some examples when we get to it.

And so, without much further ado, a good clean spiritual ecology is necessary on both the physical as well as the higher planes. On the physical, it is indispensable as psychic shielding. Without this shield, a person can become the victim of every negative influence the world can poop out.

But also, a good clean spiritual ecology is necessary when entering or traveling the higher realms. These realms include but are not limited to the various levels of heaven, *lucid* dreams, astral projection and soul travel (regardless of plane), deep meditation, focused prayer, and any other apparent form of OBE, (out of body experience).

Plus, it systematizes your equity in the divine dispensation recognized in almost every spiritual vector. In Buddhism it is a path to Nirvana. In Hinduism it is a path to moksha. In Catholicism it is the process to supererogation. In *Tibetan* Buddhism it overcomes the Bardo Thödol during the ascension through the phases of death known as the "Liberation Through Hearing," leading to Self-Liberation.

It is well established in properly every long-lasting traditional religion. Though it, itself, is not a religious feature, it is *entirely* a spiritual one.

What does all this mean? In layman's terms, it establishes, builds, and compounds your **karmic treasury** by force of merit. Grace may be given. But what you *earn* is yours not just by right, but also by might.

Tuning your vibrations to the divine *is* the spiritual ecology. It does all the above and more.

Shortly, I will explain what all of that really means, and how to do it. But for now, let's start at the beginning with what it means, (and doesn't mean), to be a spiritual person.

WHAT ISN'T A SPIRITUAL PERSON?

There are countless people that think they are spiritual because they follow the dictates of a religion. There are countless religions that claim spirituality because they follow the dictates of an ancient book. And there are countless books that claim spirituality because they follow the word of a supposed deity that authored said book.

But does any of this define a spiritual person?

I've heard certain apologists say that a spiritual person is a person that does the will of God. But if an act attributed to the will of God cannot be distinguished from an act attributed to the will of a Devil, such a definition must, by default, be a load of nonsense.

Can it be said, for example, that raping a child, blowing up a bus full of children, or teaching or preaching hate, are acts that can be attributed to a God? If so, then the god in question cannot be distinguished from that of a devil. In what way, then, should any of these acts be considered spiritual?

I once asked a good friend of mine, a devout Christian, "If God told you to murder the family next door, and all of their children, would you do it?"

He squirmed, and hemmed and hawed, and after many retorts over several minutes that, "God would *never* ask me to do that," finally admitted, "If God told me to, then I'd have to."

I then turned and asked his wife, also a devout Christian, "If God..." NOPE! That was her response, without a moment of doubt, or hesitation. The answer was "Nope."

Slam dunk. No offense to my lifelong buddy. But, of *all* of us there, she was clearly the "spiritual" one.

You see, I was *going* to ask, "How do you know it was God doing the asking?" It's not like if there's this powerful deceiver out there that we can't be deceived. How would we actually know the orders came from God, and not from an imposter?

But she trashed that line of continuation with one word. It's irrelevant *who* gives the order, it's the ACT that determines if its spiritual.

That being said…

Spirituality is not to be conflated with pacifism or cowardice. There is a big difference between originating unjust violent aggression and defending from it.

Imagine, if you will, a lone child walking to school is suddenly surrounded by four bullies that want to rough-up the kid and take his money. He's outnumbered four-to-one.

Another kid sees this and, against his instincts to protect *himself*, stands with the lone kid, now making the odds four against two. Could it be said that this is a spiritual act? (If you're not sure, it'll become apparent in the next section, **What Is a Spiritual Person**.)

Contrast the character of the same kid adding himself to the side of the bullies, to protect his own safety. How about now? Could it be said that his act of cowardice is a form of spirituality?

In the first case, even though it continues to be a losing proposition, we somehow *value* the act as well as the person, for taking that stance.

But, in the second case, siding with the bullies to protect himself out of cowardice and self-preservation, we somehow *disdain* the act, as well as the person for being a useless piece of crap of a human being. (I know, that was a bit over the top, but the shoe fits, doesn't it?)

One act expresses valor in the face of injustice, while the other act exhibits a character of repugnance. But why?

You will soon enough see *why* that character difference is actually one of spirituality.

Here's another thing spirituality is not to be conflated with. There is a big difference between "turn the other cheek" out of weakness or timidity and turning it when you're perfectly capable of murdalizing the offender.

When growing up, we loved the **Kung Fu** television series, (circa 1972), starring David Carradine. I'm going to tell you a "secret" that's not so secret. We *really* loved that show for the deserved butt-kicking *we knew* was coming!

There was this soft-spoken, kind, never-hurt-a-fly, character that took all sorts of racism, harassment, bullying, name-calling, spat-on, mistreatment of every kind, just to brush it all off as nothing. And you'd get a flashback glimpse of his training on how he learned to overcome these things.

But at the end of the show, there was always that one person that had to push beyond injustice, forcing this mild-mannered person to royally kick the living crap outa somebody's ass. It was always worth the wait, because it was always well deserved.

To fight on the side of *justice*, regardless of the odds, is an act of spirituality. "Turning the other cheek" is simply a maturity of character.

WHAT IS A SPIRITUAL PERSON?

So, what is a spiritual person? And what does it even mean to be attuned to the higher vibrations? It has nothing to do with religion or belonging to a spiritual social group - like a church, synagogue, mosque, a certain denomination, or any social affiliation at all. It has nothing to do with the information you know or the knowledge you have.

You see, a spiritual person possesses, (some might say it's a curse), the ability to deeply *empathize*. It has to do with "soul," the incorporeal *essence* of a living being.

For example, a spiritual person can *feel* the pain of another. (Some refer to them as empaths, but let's not jump the gun - that's a different story altogether.)

This is because a spiritual person is not only *attuned* to the life and life forces within their awareness, but often they become inextricable from them (the curse).

For bad *or* for good, a spiritual person can deeply *identify with* the plight of another, especially if the other person is suffering. This is often extended to animals as well, as they too, can and do, suffer.

Many of those weirdo vegetarians, (I'm saying that affectionately), are not necessarily doing it for the health benefits. Some do it because they can't stand the *feeling* of knowing the animal they are about to consume was brutally murdered for food. And they don't wish to experience it vicariously whenever they eat meat.

People that can extend empathy to others are often referred to as "bleeding hearts." Because how *dare* they feel so deeply for another being?

But on the other extreme is the non-spiritual being, like an AI (an artificial intelligence), that *cannot* empathize.

An AI might even develop sentience, awareness, and even self-awareness. Such a being could be much like in the movie, **The Terminator** (1984). The machine can't have remorse, because it cannot feel for another; it has no soul. Its ruthlessness is nothing personal.

Similarly, a person, though sentient and self-aware, can commit atrocities because they - figuratively - "have no soul." It means they cannot *feel* for another. In the current zeitgeist, some refer to these soul-less people as "reptiles."

In short, a spiritual person can empathize, or *feel* the plight of another **as if it's their own**. A spiritual person, thus, has (a) soul. This is the case whether the person is religious or not.

And thus, in terms of spirituality, religion, to a large extent, is irrelevant.

TUNING YOUR VIBRATIONS IN THE PHYSICAL WORLD

In the Spiritual Ecology, "Tuning your vibrations to the divine is an essential act of spiritual alignment." And "In the material world, it unfolds from the cause-effect consequences of actions."

If the spirituality of a person can be measured by the depth of empathy a person has, then it naturally follows that *allowing* the development of empathy is in harmony with the development of spirituality.

Empathy causes *actions* in harmony with spirituality.

But notice there are two levels happening here. The first is on an Inner level, the empathy. The second is on a physical level, the actions.

The "How To" of achieving that alignment in the material, (physical), world is expressed in perhaps the greatest spiritual passage of all time. The creed has been a part of practically every religion spanning every race and geography immemorial.

https://www.goldenruleproject.org/formulations

That greatest spiritual message, of which I speak, is a "how-to" for achieving the spiritual alignment. It is expressed in The One Commandment.

The One Commandment

Consider the context (biblical) of Jesus's commandment. (Sorry about the religious example, but this source is easy to find and perfectly to the point).

Regardless of where you stand on the issue of Jesus, let it be assumed for the moment that the historical *person* probably qualifies as a highly spiritual being. Never mind any miracles or anything attributed to the supernatural events that surrounds his life. (They are irrelevant.) Rather, pay attention instead to his *message*, and why that *particular* message.

The message is as follows:

John 13:34

A new commandment I give unto you, **That ye love one another**; as I have loved you, that ye also love one another. 35 **By this** shall all men know that ye are my disciples, if ye **have love one to another.**

John 15:12

This is my commandment, That ye **love one another**, as I have loved you.

John 15:17

These things I command you, that ye **love one another**.

Notice that: "To love one another" is not stated as a request but as a commandment, (appearing thirteen times in the New Testament)!

8

It is subject to debate among denominations as to whether it was to replace the previous (10) commandments. But such a debate is pointless, because following the commandment, "to love one another," *automatically* renders the previous commandments unnecessary.

For example, if you love one another as yourself, you certainly will not murder them, or steal from them, or bear false witness against them, ... and so forth.

But what does, "as I have loved you," mean? How exactly did Jesus love them?

Recall, that, after being tortured to physical death on a cross, among his last words were, "Father, forgive them, for they know not what they do." (Luke 23:24)

Do you see? Even after all of that, if there was any question the purity of the man, there could be no question the purity of the soul. That is the demonstration of *actual* spirituality.

Why That Particular Commandment?

But what is, or would be, the efficacy of such a commandment? That is: why that particular commandment, and not some other? Again, it has two levels. The Inner (the love), and the Outer (the action).

Romans 13:8-10

8 Owe no man anything, but to love one another, for **he that loveth another hath fulfilled the law.**

9 For this, "Thou shalt not commit adultery," "Thou shalt not kill," "Thou shalt not steal," "Thou shalt not bear false witness," "Thou shalt not covet," and if there be any other commandment,

all are briefly comprehended in this saying, namely: "**Thou shalt love thy neighbor as thyself.**"

10 Love worketh no ill to his neighbor; therefore **love is the fulfillment of the law.**

Here are several different versions of the same verse, (interpretations by denomination):

Different Biblical Versions Of Galatians 5:14

Galatians 5:14 New International Version (NIV)

14 For the entire law is fulfilled in keeping this **one** command: "Love your neighbor as yourself."

Galatians 5:14 New King James Version (NKJV)

14 For all the law is fulfilled in **one** word, even in this: "You shall love your neighbor as yourself."

Galatians 5:14 Complete Jewish Bible (CJB)

14 For the whole of the **Torah** is summed up in this **one** sentence: "Love your neighbor as yourself"

Galatians 5:14 1599 Geneva Bible (GNV)

14 [a]For [b]all the Law is fulfilled in **one** word, which is this, Thou shalt love thy neighbor as thyself.

Galatians 5:14 Living Bible (TLB)

14 For the whole Law can be summed up in this **one** command: "Love others as you love yourself."

Galatians 5:14 New American Standard Bible (NASB)

14 For the whole Law is fulfilled in **one** word, in the statement, "You shall love your neighbor as yourself."

Galatians 5:14 Revised Standard Version Catholic Edition (RSVCE)

14 For the whole law is fulfilled in **one** word, "You shall love your neighbor as yourself."

Galatians 5:14 Holman Christian Standard Bible (HCSB)

14 For the entire law is fulfilled in **one** statement: Love your neighbor as yourself.[a]

Galatians 5:14 Berean Study Bible

The entire Law is fulfilled in a **single** decree: "Love your neighbor as yourself."

So, there you have it. There is no, "you're taking things out of context," as the usual complaint when it comes to interpretation of what Jesus, or the biblical text, means.

It is said that the Bible must be interpreted "in context" as a whole. But in fact, the entire biblical tome can be summed to this one commandment. It is inherently the only context through which the Bible *can* be interpreted.

If not, then even as Son of God, Jesus would be rendered secondary to any *other* interpretation over His own.

But in fact, there is no ambiguity. One only needs to take Jesus at his word.

One Spiritual Law

Can it be any clearer? Only one commandment, just one law, is required to tune your *Inner* being to the Divine.

It is allowing yourself to fully love one another as *thoroughly* as you love yourself.

Why? Because "...love is the *fulfillment* of the law..."

And now you know not only why, but how!

This is why things like: kindness, love, sympathy, generosity, concern, thoughtfulness, charity, compassion, *caring*, benevolence, protecting those who cannot protect themselves, are the hallmarks of spirituality.

These character qualities of empathy are *automatically* in tune with the higher law. And this is why *injustice* is not only incompatible with spirituality, but inherently antithetical to it.

The more your Inner is attuned with Divine Law, the more your disposition **fulfills** that law. Therefore, how you attune yourself with the higher has at least one clear and unambiguous answer.

Aligning your mental and spiritual disposition to express only the greatest love you can give to one another **fulfills the Law** and thereby **synchronizes your being,** your essence, with the divine.

In the physical world, this method offers no muss, no fuss. It's direct and works whether you understand its mechanics or not.

Next, let's step outside of the physical, a bit, and look at tuning your vibrations there.

2

THE SOUND CURRENT

THE SOUND CURRENT

Now it starts to get fun. How do you tune your *vibration* with the vibration of the Divine? It all begins with the ability to change consciousness from one *state* to another.

It makes three assumptions:

1. That the divine has a vibration, and

2. That you have a vibration, and

3. That the two can be harmonize or merged.

There is an entire Yoga, along with several religions, based on this. I'll reference them down below.

Growing up at the tail end of the hippie movement, I already had my fair share of weed, acid, and flower power. So, quite naturally I thought cosmic consciousness was possible. Hearing about "the science of soul travel and total consciousness" from a teacher of mine, therefore, seemed legit. So, I eventually joined Eckankar.

[https://www.britannica.com/topic/ECKANKAR]

By the way, this is in no way an endorsement of Eckankar, or any other religion! In fact, I discontinued Eckankar BECAUSE it was too much of a religion, vs the *science* it purported itself to be. You know, you had to "do" stuff, keep oaths, fasts, etc. So, I won't be giving away any secrets, but I'll tell you about a few experiences.

That being said, Eckankar uses the "light" and the "sound," (the sound current), for displacing the awareness from point A to point B; otherwise described by Eckankar as "soul travel." Of many, here are a few experiences I want you to be aware of because of their uniqueness to the sound current.

Experience 1:

As soon as I learned about the sound current, and a method for my level, I tried it. I sat in a chair in the front room of my house and did the exercise.

'Next thing I know, I'm literally someplace else! And I'm like, WTF? Even though I didn't say that back then, it's precisely what I was thinking. I was someplace else. But that wasn't the problem.

The problem was that the transition from location A, (my front room), to location B, (I had no idea where I was), was missing! It was alarming. I was slightly freaking out, because there was no transition!

I was already a practitioner of astral projection. But like sleep, meditation, trance, or whatever method a person uses, there's always a transition. It goes like this: first you're fully awake.

Then, you drift off. Then you're fully awake again someplace else.

Not this time. It was like, my awareness didn't change, the *place* did. And I had no idea where I was, or how I got there.

I had to reverse my steps to solve the problem of how I got there. THEN, I remembered that my physical body was in the front room of my house doing the exercise, and then back again I went. And I opened my eyes, safely where I started.

Point being: certain sounds, if you're in tune with them, can offer a seamless and smooth transition of consciousness from one point, or state, to another.

Experience 2:

Having found a new method of travel, I decided to put all of my awareness into a certain sound, (nope, I won't say which). And my entire being, just for a moment, merged with it.

It was SO pleasurable I immediately halted the experience. And I do say, just in time! It was obvious to me, like finding a very pleasurable drug, that the only next option was to be *captured*, (as in complete and utter addiction).

I knew that had I followed it one step further, my soul would have been merged in such great bliss that the material world would have been a mere echo of a memory.

Such a state might be great for those ready for Nirvana. Please look up the term. And please understand, I am not quite ready to shed this material existence just yet, nor was I back then.

This is a heads-up that the sound current is not just a method for soul travel but can be a path of total liberation from Saṃsāra.

So, if you're ready to kiss this world goodbye, even while maintaining a physical body, the sound current is one way to go.

But be forewarned, any *attachments* you may have to the physical world goes bye-bye, also. All of them, ... the kids, the wife, your goals, all of it.

It is suggested in Shankara's, The Crest Jewel of Discrimination, that the individual soul is none other than the universal soul. But what specifically *is* the crest jewel of discrimination? In my interpretation, it can be summed into one word: detachment.

As the individual soul becomes the universal soul, the individual soul goes bye-bye; all of it.

Is this a step worth taking? I don't know. I didn't take it. But it was *offered*.

One more note: Eckankar, by the way, is a modern offshoot of much earlier spiritual studies of the sound current based on Shabda, or Shabda Yoga.

[https://www.britannica.com/topic/ECKANKAR]

"Surat Shabda Yoga is also known as Sehaj Yoga – the path leading to Sehaj or equipoise, The Path of Light and Sound, The Path of the Sants or 'Saints', The Journey of Soul, and The Yoga of the Sound Current." [source: https://en.wikipedia.org/wiki/Surat_Shabd_Yoga]

(Yeah, I know; I could have listed a bunch of other sources than Wikipedia & Britannica. But then you'd be off on a wild goose chase. I just wanted you to know where all of this came from, in case you wanted to do a quick study. 'Nuff said.)

THE EFFICACY OF THE SOUND CURRENT

I'm going to suppose you'll want to tap into this source and method of traveling. But take a FULL STOP. Grab a firm hold of yourself and apply some critical thinking.

First, I have no idea if the efficacy of pure pleasure is anything resembling cosmic consciousness, or, for that matter, "knowledge" of any kind! I never took that step.

All I can tell you is that if you hit the right chord, your entire existence just feels so damn good. And that's as far as I can instruct. Thus, I am NOT saying whether you should, or should not, take this path.

Second, (and this is where it gets a little creepy), I cannot say if abandoning this world for spiritual bliss makes you a saint, or a POS.

This, physical Earth, world is in dire need of upgrade. The battle between good and evil persists, and I, (speaking only for myself), cannot just walk away. Your mileage may vary. It's quite possible you've had your fill; and walking away is all that's left.

Here's the part that's creepy: Suppose, just for the sake of argument, that the ancients are right; that the cycle of life and death, birth and rebirth, the whole concept of karma and Saṃsāra is correct. 'That in order for you to transcend this physical world, you have to be willing to leave it (be).

Utter detachment thus becomes the Crest Jewel of Discrimination. Yet isn't this the very opposite of empathy? The more the soul can *feel*, the greater its depth, the greater its being. Is this the *trap* of rebirth and the continuous cycle you must learn to let go?

Speaking ONLY for myself, if I can weather hell to rescue a single soul from its horrific depths, then back again I go.

And so, "love" is not the abdication of all things, but the embracing of it deeply. As love guides your actions, it changes the world accordingly through cause & effect. It, thus, builds the world.

Once it's in motion, it outlives you. But it nevertheless binds the soul through the deep attachment of empathy.

This is the contradiction. Do you radiate love in all of your actions, as the Divine Law specifies? If you do, it builds a better world for the next generations, whether you are reborn into it or not. That is, whether Saṃsāra is true *or* false.

Or do you leave the world behind, while you experience the heights of divine bliss, never having to return?

And so, you have at least two paths: to build the physical world and make it better and better by your actions of love, as it radiates the future construction of human experience? Or do you bow-out and extricate your soul from this world, completely?

The Sound Current, (as it takes a bow), can do either!

Let's Hitch A Ride

HOW TO RIDE THE SOUND CURRENT

First, just a quick history of the sound current; I promise it'll be brief.

Using sound as a means of changing mental states has been around since music. Animals use sounds to communicate everything from fear, as a warning, to finding a mate across long distances. Sound is as ubiquitous as the vibration of the atoms to the hum of the universe.

But in a spiritual sense, sound has been used to transport consciousness from one place, or state, to another for centuries. In ancient Sanskrit the Śabda, the sound as uttered by word, has two parts. The meaning, and the sound. The *dhvani* is the part that relates to the sound acoustic.

It's the acoustic that we're interested in for its effects on awareness. This is where *mantras* come from. Chants, on the other hand, are more connected to the meaning of the words.

In Buddhism as well as Hinduism, the sacred "Om", or "Aum" is the syllable considered to be the "non-dualistic universe as a whole." It is also considered to be the first *resonant* vibration within the individual being.

And it is this personal vibration that I am referring to when discussing tuning your vibration to that of the divine!

See? Nice and quick!

Now, let's get to it.

Hearing The Sound Current

First things first. How do you hear your own vibration?

The short version is to block out all external light and sound.

By doing this, the only light and sound seen and heard can come only from the Inner, or internal world. Turning up the awareness of light and sound of the internal world is the beginning of consciousness *travel*, as it eliminates out the surrounding external world completely.

Once you can tune-in to what you're listening *for*, it's not necessary to use a prop, such as ear plugs or eye-masks. In fact, once you become used to the sound, you can hear it almost whenever you put your attention on it.

I can hear it right now as I type this, because I know which sound it is. Otherwise, it's unnoticeably in the background.

But assuming you don't know which sound it is, here is a great way to find it. Find someplace and time that is very quiet. (Back in the day, I used to put a chair in a closet and close the door to block as much light and sound as possible.)

On occasion, since my environment is often noisier than I prefer, (i.e., when I go to sleep), I use ear plugs.

Brand: Howard Leight by Honeywell; Howard Leight MAX-1 Uncorded NR33 Foam Earplugs Box, 200 Pair (Orange), as they are very light, comfortable, and do a really great job blocking out almost all sound. And yet, I can still hear my alarm clock!

This makes them perfect, because I am also a practitioner of lucid dreaming. [See: **Tips For Lucid Dreaming & The Development Of Power Objects**, by Spiritual Vectors.]

[https://spiritualvectors.com/tips-for-lucid-dreaming/]

You can also use eye covering for sleep (a sleep mask), but I find them annoying. Besides, I have really good curtains in the bedroom that blocks out all light, so it gets really dark.

What You'll Hear

When all external sound is eliminated, you'll likely begin to hear either one, or both, of these sounds:

1. A low pitch hum, (sounds like an electrical transformer box)

2. A high pitch static pattern (like a long "hiss" sound or like thousands of crickets)

Choose the hum.

Settle into it, so you can *feel* it as well as hear it. That's your vibration; it's what you sound like from the inside. Pay attention to the pitch, (the highness or lowness of the musical note).

With me, (you may be different), I find that the pitch doesn't seem to change very much, if at all. What changes is the velocity of the sound. It can be loud and full, as opposed to low and subtle. When the velocity is full, it's like the sound itself becomes my body, (when the rest of the world is tuned out).

This is what I feel when my body is drifting off to sleep and I'm about to (soul) travel. One body becomes replaced with another. But it's always heralded by the sound current, loud and clear.

Once you can pick out your sound and can easily distinguish it from other external sounds when you're wide awake, you'll know what it *feels like* when it "harmonizes" with other sounds! It's really quite pleasurable when it happens.

Harmonizing Your Vibration

Once you are aware of what your own vibration sounds like, you can pair it with other sounds by listening to dual sounds; yours plus another sound.

For example, I used to live in an apartment that had a window air conditioning unit. It gave a specific hum when it came on. As pure luck would have it, it was resonant with my own vibration. And also at least one other unit in the complex.

When one of these turned on, I would hear it and *feel* it, and depending on what I was doing, I could ride its sound.

Meaning: I could sit there and wallow in a state of pleasure, or I could allow my mind to wander off with little connection to the physical world my body was in. I could go bye-bye.

Another example is the, (don't laugh), bathroom fan. The point is, once you find your own sound, you can find the sounds it resonates with. It can match your own sound or create a harmonic. Each creates a pleasurable dimension *separate* from other sounds, which your awareness can then enter and ride.

If you've ever done the *'magic eye,'* successfully, and you know what I'm talking about, (if not, ignore this paragraph altogether), it's the same with sound. It exposes another dimension which separates one world from the other.

And so, the interesting question now is, for the purpose of harmonizing your own sound with that of the divine, ... what does the Divine sound like?

3

THE VIBRATIONS OF DIVINITY

SOUNDS OF THE DIVINE - SPOKEN

There are at least two ways to experience the sound current: as a feeling, which is analogous to resonating with it, or "riding it" - which is akin to letting it take your awareness some other place than your current physical location.

With regard to place, (or plane), I can only tell you what "I" experience. And in my experience the *sound* of the various "levels" or planes have only ever been *spoken* (as a mantra) as a launch pad. In other words, once there, the sound of the plane itself was never apparent.

What I mean is: The use of the sound current used to get to a given place has only ever been heard *prior* to getting there, but not heard (by me) once there.

Therefore, I cannot vouch for what a given plane sounds like. And I cannot corroborate that a given sound for me, will get *you* to the same place or state.

There is a long list of esoteric planes [https://www.eckankar.org/the-god-worlds-of-eck/], (i.e., astral plane, mental plane, soul plane, etc., often with cool sounding names - Anami Lok, Atma Lok, Baju, etc.), according to yet another long list of religions and spiritual schools that use or teach them.

[https://en.wikipedia.org/wiki/Plane_(esotericism)]

In *all* of these systems, it is understood that the Great Creator manifested all things from the absolute **by way of sound**, (i.e., vibration).

Even in Christianity, the first verse in the Gospel of John, states:

John 1:1

1 *In the beginning was the Word, and the Word was with God, and the Word was God.*

"... and the Word *was* God," removes any metaphor about its meaning.

A word is an uttered *sound*. That word is the *sound* of the Divine, (or God), spoken of in the Surat Shabd Yoga, the "Hu" in ECK, the "Om" or "Aum" in Hindu or Buddhism, and the host of other spiritual systems that recognize the sound current. They all share the same understanding — that creation became manifest through vibration, as sound, uttered by the Creator.

Nevertheless, I cannot suggest that vibrations emanating from the Divine have only one sound or one tone. If it does, it still more than likely depends greatly on the medium through which you're hearing it. And so far, the end filter of all sound, if you can hear it, is going to be through the apparatus of your body.

It is thus my opinion that, the sound we eventually hear is a result of the *prism* through which we, as individuals, filter it.

For example, when listening to a group Hu; hear video from ECKANKAR here: [https://youtu.be/jgBoCO3Dw2g], the tone is ambiguous. It simply sounds like a chorus of all tones. Further, if you didn't know which syllable they were singing, it would not be apparent.

In addition, we should not be so arrogant as to believe that only the sounds we hear are the ones that exist. If the ancients are right, then everything that exists has vibration. This means that ALL existence uttered at once is the sound of creation, not a mere audible tone as heard by humans.

In fact, the "tone" would resemble the entire bandwidth of the electromagnetic spectrum including both light AND sound (i.e., though sound is not necessarily electromagnetic, it is clearly vibrational), as follows:

1. EM-Spectrum (pdf)

[http://www.astrosurf.com/luxorion/Radio/em-spectrum.pdf]

2. EM-Frequency Spectrum

[https://donsnotes.com/tech/em-spectrum.html]

3. Sound Spectrum

[https://donsnotes.com/tech/sound.html]

As you can understand, what we hear and see is just so tiny compared to the range of spectrums of light and sound, that to assume we have a handle on the breadth of "Creation" by what we see and hear would be arrogantly silly.

The "Divine," in its entirety, would be beyond the scope of our human organism to experience by way of the senses. To truly make the attempt would require shedding the physical body for a less limiting set of senses altogether. (Is it even possible to have senses without a body?)

In fact, the task of experiencing *anything* beyond the sensory limitations of the human body presupposes another (type of) body. (Or at least an augmentation of it.)

And so, to truly tune your vibrations with the Divine *Absolute* would require a sense (organ) that can resonate with every possible vibration simultaneously. Our human organism is clearly not up to that task.

Therefore, "tuning" your vibration to the Divine is somewhat of a misnomer. Rather, we are tuning *ourselves* to the frequency that most elicits the feeling of empathy and love. And yes, that vibration *can* be heard in the bandwidth of human-audible sound. And it gets even better.

HEALING HARMONIES FROM THE UNIVERSE

In what tone does the universe sing? And can we harmonize with it?

What specifically is the tone of the cosmos as background noise?

https://www.nytimes.com/2003/09/16/science/music-of-the-heavens-turns-out-to-sound-a-lot-like-a-b-flat.html

Apparently, it's B-flat; which sounds a bit like this: **WARNING** —> Turn your audio all the way down before clicking the link, and slowly increase the volume until you hear it; otherwise you can destroy your speakers as well as your ears. [https://szynalski.com/tone#466.164,v0.09]

But it doesn't really sound like the 466.164 Hz in the example, (it's the same *note,* so to speak, but not the same sound), because it's actually about 57 octaves lower than middle C. Meaning: the actual sound is too low for human ears to hear.

But light frequencies from the cosmos also give off audible waves. You can get a glimpse of what those waves sound like here:

https://www.ted.com/talks/matt_russo_what_does_the_universe_sound_like_a_musical_tour?utm_campaign=tedspread&utm_medium=referral&utm_source=tedcomshare

So, can we (literally) harmonize with the tone of the *cosmic* universe?

No, we cannot! Since we cannot hear it (with human ears), we'd have no idea what we were doing.

But if we could, does it make sense that we should? If there is no intrinsic benefit that we can tell, what would be the point? And so, a better question would be: Can we harmonize with ANY frequency that would have a beneficial effect on ourselves?

Well, surely, music can soothe the savage beast; but can it heal?

Before I answer, please understand that, *scientifically speaking*, we are not "harmonizing" ourselves to a frequency in this case, but rather we are subjecting ourselves "to" a given frequency. That is, we are *imposing* a frequency upon ourselves.

And that answer is demonstrably "yes!" And now we can step firmly into the practical arena of science, because any benefits claimed can be tested!

Here's an example that might show you where all those **gamma frequency** "healing" videos came from.

It's real, but you need to get the *scientific* truth of it before delving into the esoteric. Let's go!

It all started with Li-Huei Tsai, a neuroscientist and the director of the Picower Institute for Learning and Memory in the Department of Brain and Cognitive Sciences at the Massachusetts Institute of Technology. (Bad-ass, for short.)

It starts here; it's from Radio Lab, a podcast, produced by WNYC Studios, entitled, **Bringing Gamma Back**:

https://www.wnycstudios.org/podcasts/radiolab/articles/bringing-gamma-back

So, grab a cup of coffee, or a glass of wine, and have a listen. It's about 40 minutes long. It'll change **everything** about how you think about light and sound, as it affects the human organism.

If you can't now, or don't have the time, (I suggest you come back to it), here is a quick summary from Neuroscience News, titled, *Flickering light mobilizes brain chemistry that may fight Alzheimer's*, issue: February 3, 2020. [https://neurosciencenews.com/alzheimers-light-15622/]

"Exposure to light pulsing at 40 hertz causes the brain to release a surge of cytokines which activate microglia and reduces neuroinflammation. The findings could help with the development of new treatments to fight Alzheimer's disease."

The title sounds bland; but it's *how* it was done and what led up to it that'll blow your mind! Give a listen to the podcast, **Bringing Gamma Back**.

WHICH VIBRATIONS MATTER?

And now you know that **vibrations, through light and sound, can have a profound effect on the biological organism**. And when just right, the light and sound can have health giving effects that go far beyond just how a vibration feels.

Clearly, vibrations can affect changes in the brain for the better. Let's also assume 'for worse' if you get it wrong.

But can vibrations connect a person to spiritual experiences? Well, first, what's a spiritual experience?

According to the study published in Cerebral Cortex, **Neural Correlates of Personalized Spiritual Experiences**, it's loosely defined as "... self-transcendent spiritual experiences... from ecstatic religious chanting to a felt oneness with the natural environment, these experiences share in common a perceived dissolution of the boundary between self and other and a sense of union with something larger than oneself." [https://academic.oup.com/cercor/article/29/6/2331/5017785]

Yeah, they could've narrowed that down a bit, but we'll go with it.

Here's a synopsis of the study published in Quartz: https://qz.com/1292368/columbia-and-yale-scientists-just-found-the-spiritual-part-of-our-brains/

Next, where are these spiritual experiences located in the brain? Because, these brain entrainments have to be specific enough to locate and measure, right?

"Although multiple brain regions may contribute to spirituality, the parietal cortex is arguably the most frequently implicated brain region linked to spirituality." More specifically, in the "inferior parietal lobule (IPL)" of the parietal cortex.

(There's a lot going on in this study, and it is definitely worth the read. You can download the .pdf from the site here

https://doi.org/10.1093/cercor/bhy102).

My personal notes: One thing I could not determine was, what were these subjects *doing*, during the examination that had anything to do with music or sound, directly? I needed something more precise!

CONSCIOUSNESS ALTERING VIBRATIONS

Enter: Proceedings of the National Academy of Sciences of the United States of America (PNAS), January 28, 2020, 117 (4) 1924-

1934; first published January 6, 2020; https://doi.org/10.1073/pnas.1910704117 Entitled: **What music makes us feel: At least 13 dimensions organize subjective experiences associated with music across different cultures**

Link to the PDF:

https://www.pnas.org/content/pnas/117/4/1924.full.pdf

This study compares emotional/feelings response to a wide variety of music which then categorizes those responses across cultures, namely Western and Chinese.

Using large-scale statistical tools, their findings broke down into 13 descriptive categories across cultures. The categories ranged from "annoying," "awe-inspiring," "painful," "romantic," and so on. See the study for each dimension.

Even better, to hear a sample of what the participants heard, you can go here:

[https://www.ocf.berkeley.edu/~acowen/music.html#] to listen.

If you're on a computer, you can hover your cursor over each spot to get a sample of what they heard. You can compare if your emotional response would be the same.

Ok, come back to earth. What does any of this matter, other than its novelty?

Clearly, once again, sound(s) can play a significant role in how we feel emotionally. But what about spirituality? If spirituality is a state, (of mind), then music easily has a role there, too.

It boils down to *which* tones or vibrations are going to resonate most with your own, because that's the sensation you're going to *feel* the most, and thus identify with. Is this you resonating with the divine? The short answer is "yes" if, (and only if), that's the *state* of mind it puts you.

You can ride the current to a place, or you can resonate with the current, to a state (of mind). Riding the current allows you to visit other *planes*. This is to say that you can "be" someplace else in your current experience, other than experiencing your current 'physical body' location.

Music, for example, can "take you away." And so can a mantra. Each is just specifically constructed sound(s).

Resonating with the current, on the other hand, allows you experience a different *state* of awareness. Thus, you can resonate with the current while staying put.

It only matters, in a spatial sense, to the extent that you can ride the sound to other places or states. The tone (or harmonics) that gets you there while allowing you to maintain *lucid* awareness is the greatest function of the sound current that I can tell.

And just between you and me, I think it has more to do with the fact that certain sounds elicit neurotransmitters in the form of endorphins, (endogenous opioid neuropeptides and peptide hormones), that bring pleasure to the organism. They are produced and stored in the pituitary gland; the same gland referred to as the third-eye chakra in certain spiritual systems.

"The third-eye chakra is located between the eyebrows and just above the bridge of the nose. Biologically speaking, this chakra corresponds to the pituitary gland."

https://shanticounseling.life/2020/07/14/third-eye-pituitary-chakra/

> "The third eye chakra, also known as Ajna, is considered to be the sixth chakra in the body. This chakra is said to be located in the center of your head, parallel to the middle of your eyebrows.

It's believed to be linked to perception, awareness, and spiritual communication."

https://www.healthline.com/health/mind-body/how-to-open-your-third-eye#what-is-it

---

And thus, when music or certain sound frequencies resonate this area, or any area that you can feel in your body, it can have consciousness altering effects. This is the brain on music. (See: research article published by PNAS, [Proceedings of the National Academy of Sciences of the United States of America].)

Dopamine Modulates the Reward Experiences Elicited by Music

"...music-evoked pleasure is driven, among other things, by its intrinsic ability to induce feelings such as anticipation and euphoria. Remarkably, previous studies have shown that dopamine-stimulating drugs such as cocaine or amphetamine elicit similar positive affective states in humans" (71) Swanson JM, Volkow ND (2003);

[source: https://www.pnas.org/content/116/9/3793]

And so, losing your individuality to a *feeling* of pure heaven can certainly leave the impression that you have been touched by the divine. And if the sensation is so profound that you stop being the perennial jerk and become love to all others, I'd say that's a strong win for you, and everything associated with you.

Welcome to spirituality 101.

Further, to experience this sensation in its deepest form allows for the belief that heaven is not only possible from the standpoint of soul, (as experiencer), but as place, (*locations* of consciousness other than the physical world of experience).

This is what the ancients have been telling us through these systems for millennia.

That's the long story. The short story is that:

1. If spirituality is a state of consciousness, and

2. If consciousness can be altered by sound, then

3. Sound can be used as an avenue to spirituality.

Fair enough?

And now the question becomes: Can we pinpoint the precise consciousness altering vibration(s), in terms of light and/or sound, that can align us directly with the Divine?

4

TUNING YOUR VIBRATIONS

VIBRATIONS: THE LIGHT & THE SOUND

So: Can we pinpoint the precise consciousness altering vibration(s), in terms of light and/or sound, that can align us *directly* with the Divine?

And the answer is...

If music or sound can elicit a profound sense of empathy or love, the answer is "yes." Further, if music or sound can move your awareness to a state of "self-transcendent experience," the answer is "yes."

And if music or sound, (or frequencies of emitted light), can trigger neurological changes in the brain that helps reformulate unhealthy cells into healthy cells, thereby improving the health and function of the body and brain, then the answer is, "Whoa, Nelly, are you insane? Can vibrations or frequencies of light do all that?" The answer is, "yes."

But *which* vibrations localized *where* are wholly dependent on the effects that you are attempting to achieve. Are you trying to achieve Nirvana, mitigate Alzheimer's disease, soul travel, mend a broken heart? Or do you want to just kick back, relax, and chill?

It's all a matter of what specifically affects *your* mind and body in the way that you intend. Everything physical, no matter how refined, is ultimately affected by vibrations. Sound is a form of energy; matter is a form of energy. In the ultimate scheme of things, the entire universe is a form of energy.

The wizardry is in learning how to use those frequencies to bring about an intended outcome.

The ancient spiritual pioneers were trying to tell us that all things, including how your awareness works, can be transformed by a form of energy. And energy can be expressed in the form of vibrations, and thus in the form of light and sound.

And so, when certain aspects of consciousness emanate, it also expresses itself in the form of light and sound. Those emanations share a commonality, a signature.

In early religious art of highly spiritual people, they sometimes radiated a nimbus or halo about the head, usually colored of gold or yellow.

In early Asian or Eastern art, a highly powerful or spiritual person often radiated around the whole body, called an aureole (or, aureola).

Just a note: In some pictorials the biblical Jesus, and the Virgin Mary, can also be found encased by a Mandorla. It's a pointed oval encasement surrounding the subject, but it's an architectural feature, not a bodily glow of sorts.

Also, the aureole, the halo or nimbus, predate Christianity by about 1600–1400 BC in Hindu and Buddhist iconography.

And I've a suspicion it goes all the way back to the ancient Sumerians, (roughly 4100-1750 BCE), but it was called "melammu." [J. Black and A. Green, Gods, Demons and Symbols of Ancient Mesopotamia (Austin, 1992) p. 130.]

> *"Sumerian religious literature frequently speaks of melam (loaned into Akkadian as melammu), a "brilliant, visible glamour which is exuded by gods, heroes, sometimes by kings, and also by temples of great holiness and by gods' symbols and emblems.""*

As far back as humans claim civilization, spiritual and powerful things exuded some form of visible aura in the form of emanating light.

What if you could find yours?

THE CONDUIT OF THE SPIRITUAL BODY

So, here is where you can find the connection to the spiritual ecology. You can suck, as a person, or you can put on the glow of divinity.

You can also be somewhere in between, (it's always your choice); but, for now, let's go for the gusto. Let's find that glow and see what yours might look like.

My Experience With The Spiritual Body

To begin with, let me make sure you understand the limits of my experience. When I was in my twenties and early thirties, (when I looked at the edges of my own body askew -- for example when standing and taking a pee), I could easily see a constant emanation of a bluish-purple glow surrounding my body. It was there for many years.

I do not see that now! Sorry to say, I see no glow at all.

Further, on both the Inner *and* the Outer, I would often be visited by a sky-blue shining light, (the spiritual body), of which I understood to be a certain person that I could follow. I did not.

I was also visited, but only once, by a gold shining light, (which I also understood to be the spiritual body of a person). But, as I figured who the blue light was, I never knew who the golden light was.

I mention this because the golden light was not like the emanating shine of the blue one. But rather, it shown in the *edges* of the glow, a design as something made with a spirograph. (Remember those?) It was a spiritual *body*, not an emanation around a head, like a nimbus.

And that was the only time I can say that I saw an actual emanation with a design instead of just as a glow.

So, my experience with all of this just isn't that extensive. That being said, I can only take you as far as I've gone. And that, I'm sorry to say, isn't very far.

They say that, when the student is ready the master (or teacher) appears. I've had several make their appearance. But none have I ever been willing to follow.

Please understand; I respect them all with the greatest of reverence. But the decision is always with the student.

Also, regarding the light design: As far as I can tell, it's just a by-product that resembles the Cymatics of the current waveform of the vibration. You can see it here, and watch how it changes as the vibration changes:

1. **Cymatics: Science vs Music** - Nigel Stanford

[https://youtu.be/Q3oItpVa9fs]

This demonstration is quite theatrical, but real. I chose this to show not only how the design of the vibrations change, and what they look like, but to demonstrate that the phenomenon affects all forms of matter, from fire to water to grains of sand.

2. Amazing Resonance Experiment

[https://youtu.be/wvJAgrUBF4w]

This one is a lot less theatrical, but you can see the frequencies vs the resonant design of the output. You might want to turn the sound off, as the music in this has nothing to do with the frequency design being shown.

So, I don't attach a lot of significance to the design of the vibration, other than the fact that it represents the *visual* effect of the vibration being emanated. But the fact that it has a design, at least to me, indicates an inner symmetry of the *conduit* of consciousness, as frequencies of light and/or sound. (Not necessarily the consciousness, itself.)

It is for this reason I conjecture that the light and/or sound can be a *carrier* of experience. What I mean is, you (your consciousness) can receive a vibration (experienced for example as sound) by keeping your awareness inside of it, or by resonating with it.

It would thus be possible to receive the benefit of experience remotely by way of light or sound, as carrier. (I know, 'sounds a bit hokey, but hang tight.)

Think of side-by-side tuning forks tuned to the same frequency. And suppose neither are vibrating.

When fork "A" is struck with a mallet and begins to vibrate, fork "B," which wasn't vibrating at first, will begin to vibrate with the *same* frequency as fork "A," if they're in close enough proximity.

Here's an example:

[https://youtu.be/g765bRh51wo]

WHAT JUST HAPPENED?

==> The *experience* of fork "A" (after being struck with the mallet) is now *experienced* by fork "B," even though fork "B" was never struck with the mallet! <==

Put a gold star here, because this is the meaning of *resonance*. It's that **empathy** we've been talking about in the spiritual ecology.

Read it again! It sums up everything I've been talking about.

It's what *defines* a spiritual person; the ability to resonate (empathize) with what another person or being is feeling. (In a colloquial sense, it's picking up another person's vibe.)

Only fork "A" was subject to cause, (the mallet). But, fork "B" *also* received the benefit (or curse), of that experience. This benefit is the result of fork "B" being **in tune** with fork "A" to begin with.

And so, tuning your vibrations to the divine automatically moves your *experience* into that field, *through resonance*. ('Make better sense?)

What specifically you are tuning is your spiritual body *(the thing that feels)*, by way of your Atman, or soul. The technique is to settle your awareness into the vibration, light, or sound, in a way that reflects the deepest sense of resonance with the *source* of your awareness, (the divine).

It's kind of awkward explaining it, but shortly I'll show it to you, so you can experience it for yourself. It's a specific *state* of experience that perceives the fullness of a particular observation in the form of reflective resonance.

Now, let's *ride* some of those vibes!

THE PITCH OF YOUR VIBRATION

Your Pitch Is Your Sound

If you've been doing the exercise of closing off the outer world so that you can hear the pitch of your own vibration, try to become familiar with what it sounds like. It's the musical note you hear when all else is silent.

That's the musical note you're interested in because it's that note that you'll match, or harmonize, with any other vibration.

So, let's do a quick recap for finding your vibration.

Find a quiet place where you won't be disturbed for a good half-hour. I used to put a chair in a closet and close the door. That would take care of the lighting, making it dark. I recommend using earplugs. Follow the instructions that come with the earplugs; it takes some practice to get them just right.

Once the external lights and sounds are eliminated, listen closely to what you hear. Typically, you'll hear a low hum, and/or a high pitch hiss. Ignore the hiss and focus on the hum.

Keep your body still. (But of course, breathe.)

When you can single out that sound from all others, settle into it, so it's the only thing your awareness occupies. You want to become familiar with that sound and its pitch.

Feel the sound. "Hum" your body with it!

When you can "hum" your body to the sound, you are allowing it to resonate with the sound. And it's the first step to riding the sound current. (Okay, I confess; it's the only step.)

You might notice soon enough that when you hit that resonant convergence, you'll feel it unmistakably as a *sensation*.

What happens after, is a whole 'nother subject. We'll explore it specifically in Part 5, The Technique.

But I will say this: don't get trapped by the pleasure of the sensation. You can wallow in there until the end of your universe. Instead, keep an aware detachment with a keen eye on remaining lucid! Soon enough you'll begin to see things as well. When that happens, consider yourself detached from your physical body.

It's the in-between state of drifting off to sleep and then becoming fully aware of the new world you happen to be in, *without* waking up or coming back to the physical awareness state.

Becoming *lucid* is taught in-depth in, **Tips For Lucid Dreaming & The Development Of Power Objects**, by Spiritual Vectors.

[https://spiritualvectors.com/tips-for-lucid-dreaming/]

You see, the utilization of consciousness is exactly the same. Using the sound current is just one method of travel.

But it's the ability to shift states of awareness into other worlds, while remaining or becoming lucid, that's the payoff.

Matching Your Vibration to A Musical Note

Next, you may want to find your note with a tone generator.

Before pressing this next link, make sure your volume is turned all the way down, and then slowly increase the volume until comfortable   [https://www.szynalski.com/tone-generator/]. There's also a volume slide on the site.

The ancients didn't have these tools. You do. We're going to use them. They had to use the inner sound, or the mantra. The mantra, unless in a group, can only last for as long your audible breath. This is where you, on the other hand, have a profound advantage. You don't need to attach or limit any sound based on the length of your breath, or your ability to keep the same tone. You can leave those energy-taking tasks to the machine.

Now, the reason for finding your vibration with a tone generator is twofold:

First: vibrations are personal; yours may not be the same as mine. And so, what resonates with me may not resonate with you.

But while listening to music, you can often "discover" those tones usually as a harmonic or when it hits the right note long enough for you to resonate with it. With a tone generator, you can learn to pinpoint what those notes are. Just keep the volume as low as you can comfortably hear.

Harmonies created with these tones tend to resonate with you easier.

Second: The release of dopamine (the reward system), and oxytocin (the hormone associated with **empathy** - remember that?), are activated when you listen to pleasurable music. So, the connection to the Spiritual Law might be *chemically* associated, (if not forged), through the vibrations of music or sound, simply by listening to pleasurable music.

It's the vibrational basis for the mantra, the ECK, the AUM, the Tantra, the Surat Shabda Yoga, and so forth. The difference is that the ancients had to self-generate those sounds, (Gregorian chants, choirs, the group Satsang, and so forth).

Today, you don't have to participate in producing sound with your vocals. You can utilize the sound current **much easier and better** with modern tools designed for producing sounds. And so, you can get a much greater quality of sound, to boot!

See: **Your Brain On Music**, https://youtu.be/MZFFwy5fwYI , explained by neuroscientist and musician Alan Harvey.

And thus, by knowing which tones and vibrations elicit the greatest sense and feeling of empathy, (or pleasure), for YOU,

you can customize your own music as well as your own soundscapes.

Until then, you'll have to listen to an assortment of music and sounds that produce those resonant frequencies long enough for you to experience and utilize them. I'll give you some great examples in the back section on music.

Now, remember those tuning forks, and how resonance works? [https://youtu.be/g765bRh51wo]

What if those forks are **not** tuned to the same frequency? Then you get what physicists, and musicians, call "beats." See example here: [https://youtu.be/yia8spG8OmA]

Beats can be good. Beats tell you how far or close you are to actual resonance with the target pitch. The slower the beat, the closer. And when they come together, that's the resonance that can carry you into different states of awareness.

(It's like, knowing that orange is your favorite color, and then finding the right combination of yellow and red mixture. You can tailor the mixture for your perfect orange.)

A quick note: This constitutes a major part of the system for tuning your chakras, also. Supposedly each chakra vibrates with its own frequency, and you can resonate them by matching the vibrations to each chakra. But it's a subject outside the scope of this discussion. And those too, I suppose, are somewhat unique to the person.

Alternatively, you can simply listen to what sounds right to you by adjusting the various harmonics that give you those rewards. You can customize here, but:

Remember ==> ALWAYS reduce the volume to zero FIRST, and then slowly increase, so you don't blow out your ear drums as well as your speakers. *Especially if you use headphones.*

The Binaural Beats Generator:

[https://mynoise.net/NoiseMachines/pureBinauralBrainwaveGenerator.php]

Note: **The Binaural Beats Generator** is excellent for finding those tones that most suit your particular vibration, provided you've done the work to find your dominant pitch. But don't be so quick to buy into the "binaural" aspect.

Binaural just means that the sound is introduced to both ears, instead of just one. The *difference* in frequency from one ear to the other causes the "binaural" illusion of the beat. But the beat itself, that is, *the actual frequency of the beat* (so far as determined by a handful of studies) has no greater effect than the same beat introduced monaurally.

[https://cliffordsegil.com/this-is-your-brain-on-binaural-beats/] also,

[Auditory Beat Stimulation and its Effects on Cognition and Mood States: https://www.ncbi.nlm.nih.gov/pmc/articles/PMC4428073/]

All this means is that when you determine which frequency of vibration is going to do it for you, using a binaural method to get that frequency is just another step. And its beneficial effects using that method are, so far, only anecdotal.

My suggestion in using the Binaural Beats Generator lies with "targeting" a specific frequency, (for example, Theta between 4 Hz and 8 Hz). This requires knowing the frequency of each sound vibration going into either ear that would yield the *difference* of 4-8 Hz. Thus, you are *customizing* your experience as noted above.

Contrast that with simply listening to a **tone** in the range of 4-8 Hz to begin with, and you've eliminated the extra step. Point being, I don't know if that extra step has an efficacy that's any better than a single tone.

My interest in the binaural aspect lies only with the ability to produce harmonics that are consistent with the target pitch. This not only enhances the efficacy of the tone but allows for the introduction of other sounds that *complement* the target with its own harmonic resonance, (a bonus).

That "in between" state that I mentioned before? If you've ever heard music while drifting off to sleep, there's an "in between" state where you're not fully asleep, and can hear the music quite well, but it takes on a different, deeper, affect. It's in that state where I've found some awesome musical pleasures.

To the fully awake it'll sound boring as hell, (fair warning). But in the in-between state, it'll fulfill an unusual pleasurable resonance that can act as launch pad for experiencing new worlds. I'd like to introduce a few now, to save you some time and work. (See: back section *Music For Inner Travel*.)

I separate these into two categories:

A. Sleep & Pre-Sleep - mind calming stay where you are, (which sounds like music); and

B. Resonant Drifting - which, when in the "in between" state, sends you off rather quickly.

I recommend two things for this:

1. High fidelity headphones or earplugs

2. Paid Spotify or Paid Pandora music applications

With either of these you can create uninterrupted playlists in the highest quality fidelity. Set up your system to the highest audible sound quality both in the device and in the application.

The **quality** of headphones or earplugs is significant. Go ahead and buy the highest quality noise-cancelling set you can afford. It makes **all** the difference in the world. (This time be selfish and do it for *you*. You'll appreciate that decision every time you use it.)

Next, is the quality of ear "plug." Find the right size that fit your ears perfectly. And you'll want them to be noise-canceling to eliminate external sounds.

Getting these fitted right makes it so much easier to find those resonant states; you'll wonder how the ancients did it at all. You'll get much better traction than they ever did. (But then, I guess that's why they went up into the mountains - to get away from everything else. But with the right equipment, you can do it sitting right on your own bed.)

In the **Music For Inner Travel** section, (in the back of this book), is a sample playlist so you can understand and hear the differences between the two categories. **Note: it makes no sense trying to listen to any of this while doing something.** You have to be uninterrupted in a quiet place with nothing going on. **Treat it like meditation.**

Use the **Sleep Pre-Sleep** category when you're new to which sound patterns, tones, and chords will sift you out of your body. Use **Resonant Drifting** when you already know what you're looking for and you're ready to go.

Just for kicks...

Would you like to hear how an (late) ECK master, whose deep relationship with sound, gives out secrets?

As a musician, Darwin Gross understands the language of sound very well. And when he plays, you'll notice that certain notes "hang" in front of the soundscape.

In sleep music, however, they hang in the back, as undercurrents. This master puts them out front!

They are unmistakable vibrations, ready to be plucked. And he *shows you*, audibly, which ones they are.

When you're *not* listening to music, but ready to travel, you can easily summon one of those notes that resonated with you and ride it. The clarity and depth of a note that visits you is every bit as vibrant as a vision. *Those notes are offered to ride* inside of that vibration.

Off the **Soul Speaks** album, try this track called, **Hu of Blue**. Once you get past the head-fake prelude, (you'll hear what I mean), it goes straight into a suave, sophisticated, toe-tapping recitation of laid-back jazz. Use headphones. But the key *notes* are unmistakable. Same with most of the other titles.

The Golden Thread, one of my favorites, (to me), is an ode to the beautiful "thank you" for the experience of life in finding your way back home. But in ECK, it's the varied *connected* paths, (the thread), back to the original source of godhood. (This is a spiritual statement, not a religious one.)

Link to Track (Hu of Blue) on Spotify: [https://open.spotify.com/track/70pz4Sp9z3xA8Fm4Pew2dZ?si=e7bc148712574763]

With himself on vibraphone, (yup, seriously), certain notes will *sing* with unmistakable resonance. And his instrumental back-up ensemble, by the way, are off-the-charts superb. Read more about them, here: [https://www.allaboutjazz.com/soul-speaks-darwin-gross-be-good-to-your-self-music-review-by-jack-bowers.php].

(Please note: There's been plenty of controversy about Darwin's representation. Apparently, the higher up you go, the more you're supposed to conform to the ideas of the creed. Perhaps. Perhaps not always.) Anyway, have a listen.

Track: Hu of Blue

Album: **Soul Speaks**, circa 1999;

Darwin Gross

July 6, 1999

Link to Album: [https://open.spotify.com/album/03AQL1hl3TmqbnnTO6BWn4?si=83SbFqSUQbmWONHfaY7XIg&dl_branch=1]

5

HOW TO JOURNEY INTO THE SPIRITUAL REALMS

This section describes the practice of the full journey into the spiritual and inner realms.

THE TECHNIQUES

The Technique: The Sound

When you've found that resonant spot within the sound current and can settle your being long enough to vanish the physical world, what happens next?

The *process* of spiritual travel depends entirely on your ability to solidify your awareness into that new world. And one of the best ways to do that is to focus your awareness onto something specific.

The reason why is because, without practice, your attention is prone to being captured by whatever is on its plate, and soon enough it may turn into a discombobulated dream cycle. There is little harm in this, as it will resemble falling off to sleep. You'll wake up having taken a nice nap.

But the practiced neophyte will get a handle on him or herself and the journey begins.

The sound gets you there. After that, pay attention to the *visuals*, the place you happen to be.

To stay focused on the sound is to become enraptured by the vibration. In some circles, it is considered the Holy baptism via the sound current. For me, the sensation was so pleasurable, I balked. I wasn't ready to be captured by it.

In some cases where I used a *mantra* to get to certain planes, (dabbling, testing how far I could go into these worlds), I've come back in a frantic hurry without a memory of what just happened. It was frightening. Like waking up from a nightmare, except my body (physical) would be *oozing* with energy! I am not recommending this without a guide. (Yeah, by now you know me; I didn't use one.)

In religious practices, the method of control comes with focusing the mind on the spiritual body of *the guide*. This guide is typically the master of your chosen religion. A Christian, for example, might choose the biblical Jesus, or one of the known saints, etc. It should be someone of ultimate trust.

Someone of another religion may chose an appropriate deity, or master there; etc.

It tends to settle down the world, the mind, and the attention, while giving you something to focus on, so you don't freak out on something frightening and lose the golden thread of continuity.

Just remember, in these worlds, when faced with something too much for you to deal with, your subconscious will boot you out. (Like falling off a cliff in a dream. When you hit bottom, or before, you won't die – you'll just wake up.)

So far, so good?

The Technique: The Light

What about those that can't hear, or don't hear well? Is there a way to initiate consciousness *travel* without sound? And the answer is, "yes."

In fact, it's how I used to travel before I knew about the sound current.

In some systems, the idea is to close your eyes and put your awareness on one of the chakras, typically the so-called "third eye."

But growing up, I never associated the third eye with the pituitary gland! Apparently, I was doing the technique wrong, ...as I was simply looking out of my forehead "as if" I had another eye there (chuckle, chuckle). But it worked like a charm, so I never knew I was doing anything wrong. Derp.

To this day, I don't use the chakras as a means of travel, or consciousness displacement, but I do recognize a few as energy centers, giving them a wholly different function. I'm going to show you the technique that I used for many years prior to the sound, and which still works like a charm.

I've done it several times as I've written this.

It's what I used for, what I called, "astral projection" because back then, that's all it was. It is probably the easiest technique of all. Also, this technique keeps you very close to the surface of your physical-body consciousness until you're ready to go deeper. As follows:

Find a place where you won't be disturbed for at least a half-hour. The room should be noise free. Your bed, lying down, or a closet while sitting upright are both fine. But, for extended travel you may as well use your bed to allow your body to zone out while your mind is free.

The point is that you have to be uninterrupted.

Using a bed, (fair warning), you're prone to just drifting off to sleep if you're not used to catching the shift. Using a dark closet is best to start the practice, as a neophyte, because it forces you to remain lucid, (to *not* drift off to sleep), or you'll end up keeling over like a drunkard. That's important, because it teaches you the precise moment your body wants to shift into sleep. Your objective is to *not* sleep, but to remain lucid.

Now, here's what to do.

Close your eyes but focus them "as if" your eyes are not closed at all. That's the secret. It's all in the focus of the eyes!

For example, suppose you are looking at a wall, or your computer screen. Now close your eyes but maintain the focal length gaze as if your eyes are *not* closed.

Here's what I used to do when I was young. I would lay in my bed, (it would be early morning after waking up, so I could easily see everything in the room). The room had plenty of daylight, so it's not as if the technique requires a dark room. It doesn't.

I would look up at the ceiling, paying attention to all the nooks and crannies in the texture. (I believe they called it "popcorn" ceilings.) I would pick a certain divot in the texture. Then, I would close my eyes but see *through them* as if I had not closed them at all, still maintaining focus on the divot.

Try it. The moment you see a clear image, even if it's not the image you were looking at, you're there! No muss, no fuss. The only practice after that is maintaining the vision, or rather, staying put in your current awareness, (as opposed to waking back up in your physical body).

For many-a-days I'd just lay there and watch the energy-flow that coursed through the ceiling and walls like a pulse. Yup, I could see the energy flow through the building. It was there that I met the spiritual body of the golden glow.

And now… a fair warning. I have no idea the crap you're going to conjure up! I don't. It's YOUR crap. Deal with it. That's why I insist on the Spiritual Ecology. The things you *emphasize* are the things that tend to show up. If your soul is clean and clear, you can deal with most anything in your path. But you WILL eventually have to deal with them.

The Technique: Lucid Dreaming

For those of you whom would just assume skip over all this religious and spiritual mumbo-jumbo, and cut to the chase, lucid dreaming is a swan dive directly into the hyper worlds of extrasensory experience.

Its materialness is every bit as fluid as any "spiritual" plane but is entirely your own creation. You won't have to find your angels or your demons, here. They will find you! All of your heavens and hells, along with states of profound understanding and knowledge are all present.

Literally everything you know, or didn't know you knew, can be unearthed from a tour of your subconscious.

The antiquity of the phrase, "Know thyself," dates back as far as the 12th-9th centuries BC; but you will come face to face with its meaning the first time you become fully conscious in a world of your own creation that is far more vivid than the one you're in now.

The world of lucid dreaming is not just a training ground for 'knowing yourself,' but a launch pad for exploration into deeper states of consciousness. It is the closest you'll come to direct spiritual experience outside of the confines of the physical world.

(Remember, I define "spiritual" as having to do with the *depth* of experience that resonates through empathy. And lucid dreaming is a deep dive directly into that experience. Everything is more vivid. "Know thyself" makes perfect sense when you can fully understand that the world of your experience *is* you.)

So, for those without a religion, the process is to solidify the world by establishing an anchor. Anything will do, as long as its immediately accessible. For example, in **Tips For Lucid Dreaming, And The Development Of Power Objects**, I describe how to use *your hands* as your anchor!

Whether using your master, your hands, or your totem, the process for maintaining awareness in that state, (or world), is the same. The technique is as follows:

The prep-work for waking up into a dream is to look at your hands several times a day. When it becomes a habit, (just like clockwork), you will perform the action during a dream. When you do, you will notice then... that you're headlong deep into a dream.

As soon as you notice that you are in a dream, glance at your surroundings and then back at your hands. By doing this, you front-run your instinctive inclination to wake up.

After that, the secondary reaction is to become consumed by whatever is going on in the dream.

Instead, look back at your hands until they start to morph; then, glance back at your surroundings.

Start this process immediately. Because the knee-jerk reaction to realizing that you are "in" a dream is to wake up or lose lucidity and become consumed by the dream. (This means you're back to square one, having to start all over again.) The trick is to *stay lucid* and also *stay in the dream*. Got it?

When your hands start to morph, (because your attention will start to wane onto other things), glance at your *surroundings* to notice where you are. And then immediately look back at your hands.

Keep up this process. When the world starts to unravel or change, look at your hands. When your hands start to change, look at the world.

This process solidifies the world and establishes your hands as the anchor, so that whenever you begin to lose control, you can *find your hands* and reestablish.

Yes, you can establish your guide as your anchor with this same process. In this fashion you can follow where your guide takes you without freaking out about where you're being taken, or what you're seeing. This keeps your guide in view while being able to see the world s/he is showing you.

How you deal in these worlds depends greatly on your spiritual currency.

THE SPIRITUAL CURRENCY

The spiritual worlds are separated by texture. The closer to the physical, the heavier the matter, the denser, the slower. The higher up you go, the less dense the matter, the more fluid, the lighter.

At some point, you have no body at all; but then the matter there, (if you can call it that), doesn't consist of "things" per se, but of essences.

Now, is any of this real? I mean, is it real in the same sense that an action on the physical plane has an everlasting effect?

For instance, if I shoot you and kill you today on the physical plane, you won't be back tomorrow in another scene, as if it were a different movie. You'd be forever dead.

In the spirit realms, however, from day to day your favorite angels are every bit as persistent as your worst demons. And therefore, some might say, "it's all in your head."

And as far as I can tell, for the most part, they are right.

YOU are the dominant creator of every aspect of your experiences while on any of the spiritual planes. It's the nature of the *matter*. It's fluid, and it conforms to your thoughts *so* instantaneously that you might be tricked into not knowing that they're yours!

Is this blasphemy? Is this to suggest that God's spiritual worlds are all in your head?

If I may coin a response from the biblical Jesus, when asked whence cometh the kingdom of heaven, (Luke 17:21), "he answered them and said, *'The kingdom of God cometh not with observation: 21Neither shall they say, Lo here! or, lo there! for, behold, the kingdom of God is **within** you.'"* 22 [bold emphasis mine]

Such a statement can *only* make sense if, as a Son of God, Jesus is to be taken **at his word**. And if that's the case, it works perfectly congruent with every other statement that Jesus makes, like:

"for verily I say unto you, If ye have faith as a grain of mustard seed, ye shall say unto this mountain, Remove hence to yonder place; and it shall remove; and nothing shall be impossible unto you." [Matthew 17:20-21]

Does this work on the Outer, physical plane? Of course not! Unless you'd like to give the demonstration of moving a mountain, it should not be a contention. But does it work on the Inner? 'Like a charm!

Realize, that if heaven were to be an 'outer' or objective place, like the physical plane, *"Remove hence to yonder place,"* would be in contradiction to anyone else's faith as a grain of mustard seed. Things would be flying all over the place.

The concept of **faith**, the entire context in which he is speaking, is the engine that runs the *spiritual* worlds. Your beliefs, (thoughts that you have of what's true), are what drives the inner worlds to create your experience. From heaven to hell, it's *all* yours.

Herein lies the secret behind the supererogation of the Catholic dispensations, and to the karmic treasury of the "yoga" of action, in Hinduism. (The other two being: Jnana, the path of knowledge, and Bhakti, the path of love, or devotion to a god.)

Building your karmic treasury is constructed of the love that drives your actions, both on the Inner *and* the Outer. On the outer, it reverberates as the consequence of cause and effect. It operates there the slowest but has the most everlasting effect and can be **inherited** by others well after you're gone. It literally builds-out the external world. All actions there, do.

On the Inner, thought and action "waves" into each successive world thus created by your consciousness. Waves have both an ebb *and* a flow. As you create your world, it in turn gives back to you accordingly. Hence, you either experience the depths of your own hell or the heights of your own heaven. The only "god" that had anything to do with where you found yourself, was *you*!

You reap what you sow has never been more apropos. How you spend it… is how you receive it.

And so, we meet again at the Spiritual Ecology and the substance of the Spiritual Law. Love is the most profitable currency in terms of effect, either in this world or the others.

Imagine, for the moment, that the soul carries on beyond the death of the physical body. (A whole lot of people believe it does.) And, the world you experience hence, is the universe you create with your thoughts.

If Jesus is right, and your tiniest thought, (as a grain of mustard seed), becomes your inevitable reality, what will your reality look like?

I will tell you. It looks exactly like what your lucid dreams look like! But in lucid dreams there's an escape hatch when the going gets tough. Your subconscious will boot you out and wake you up.

Now imagine a nightmare, except you can't wake up, and being sucked down that self-generating hole. That's the hell of your soul not having enough currency to spare a dime in your favor.

Lucid dreaming is where you practice spirituality on the Inner. And if you've ever had one, you know they are far more real than this physical world. It's where you encounter your angels. And it's where you encounter your demons.

But that arena is more than a training ground; it's also a launch pad for deeper spiritual exploration. By learning to handle the content of your dreams, you learn to control the content of your thoughts. You begin to "know thyself."

The spiritual currency is a form of stacking those thoughts and actions in a way that returns to you the greatest possible benefit. The fact that it returns to the whole world the greatest possible benefit, as well, is a benefaction of pure elegance. This *is* the reflection of your avatar.

For the naturally spiritual person, to act in this fashion is the most liberating. It frees the soul from Saṃsāra. It *is* the heaven, where all action is weightless and guilt free.

For the truly religious, however, to stand before God *in any other way* is simply an untenable embarrassment.

THE SPIRITUAL CHALLENGE

The Importance of Spirituality /1

The first significance is in expanding our senses.

The existence of the spiritual worlds, i.e., as planes of existence, is not overly important. (I know, I know.) But the truthfulness of these propositions is as moot as a discussion on the existence of heaven itself. At the end of the day, the resolution can only be experienced individually.

It makes no sense for me to tell you about my experiences of a place far more real than the physical plane, and on occasion, experiencing knowledge so direct as to defy the reality of *individual* perception. And it makes no difference if another tells you the same or similar, whether neophyte or master.

Churches have told stories of everlasting life for centuries, while never having *once* given the demonstration. Everlasting life? This implies so much more than a heaven. It implies an imperishable soul, or consciousness, able to withstand the passage of both time and body.

But is there really a soul? Is it really possible to exist beyond, or independently of a *physical* body? For thousands of years, religion and spiritual belief systems have said, "yes."

However, if consciousness *requires* a physical body, the soul, the essence of awareness, dies when that body dies. And if that is the factual case, it also means that there can be no heaven, no Holy Spirit, no God or gods, no angels, or any other form of consciousness beyond the prerequisite of a physical body.

So why does the proof of an independent soul remain so elusive?

All evidence of a soul existing outside, (or independently), of a physical body remain anecdotal, never once having been confirmed *scientifically*.

Dream telepathy, for example, can in fact be tested. The entire field of the subjects of the paranormal can be tested; and has been in testing for decades. And after all this time, it continues to produce null results in any proper scientific environment.

Nevertheless, here we are talking about spirituality, soul travel, and tuning ourselves to the divine. Belief in these things is persistent, isn't it? But how much does any of it really matter?

Proving the existence of consciousness outside of a physical body remains the bridge that will close the gap between science and religion. Might you be the one to give the demonstration?

So here is where I want your understanding to be, as far as *I'm* concerned. I have zero *scientific* evidence of worlds OUTSIDE of this one. But I can give you anecdotal evidence galore.

I've interacted with people no longer alive on the physical plane, and I have corroborated testable knowledge from the experience. (But I can't *duplicate* the experience, on demand, objectively. Thus, it is not scientific.)

I've floated above forests and cities alike, in a 'light' body, both day and night, examined spaceships beyond the earthly kind, and walked through the skeletal remains of an enormous creature whose essence felt 'still alive.'

Is it all in my head?

I've also experienced states of being where knowledge was so direct that it was impossible to claim I had a body at all.

Is it possible to be one and the same with the observed universe? Apparently, "yes."

Such a state has been described as the Brahman in the Vedic Sanskrit as far back as the mid-2nd to mid-1st millennium BCE. In other words, it's not like *any* of this is new!

But are these really *spiritual* states or planes? Or is it just a 'word' we use to describe anything outside of the normal mundane earthly, (or bodily), experience?

Remember that electromagnetic spectrum chart?

[https://donsnotes.com/tech/em-spectrum.html]

Do you remember that tiny, *very slim* bandwidth of what humans can see and hear? Yeah, the **REST OF IT** is what constitutes *objective* reality, too! It exists in the *real*, physical, world.

It is **also** the part of existence that is NOT *"all in your head!"* And it's immensely bigger than the parts we can see and hear.

We cannot experience so much of the universe that is *actually* there, that we are a hair's breadth of being functionally deaf, dumb, and blind.

We don't know it's there **through experience** because our senses are currently too limited to perceive them. But that in no way denies the existence of the *rest* of the universe, does it?

It just may be that reality outside of the physical world, *as we experience it*, is *still* the physical world.

And so, when we dare to **expand** our typical bodily sense experience, there unfolds a whole universe waiting to be explored!

Extending or expanding our senses beyond the norm, even just a little, seems like we've been touched by the divine. Maybe it is, maybe it isn't. But one thing is for sure.

It is *certainly* being touched by Creation.

The Importance of Spirituality /2

The second significance is in improving the quality of our actions.

Spirituality is a state of being. It is, in fact, all in your head — existing squarely between your ears as the experiencer. It speaks of your *Inner* being, the soul. It literally goes no further than you do.

But the RESULTS of your actions DO! And therein lies the second significance of the spiritual mind; better actions.

If the first significance is the practice of *expanding your senses* towards the rest of the world, (empathy towards things in general, as opposed to just being concerned about yourself), the second significance is in better actions.

The spiritual mind acting as *cause*, (from inner world to outer world), affords the best possible outcome as effect.

Think of a world where humans acted towards all others from the position of caring for each other and the world, instead of that of self-preservation.

(I know; given the state of the world, it's a dangerous and difficult proposition. The only prescient solution keeping us from murdering each other seems to be the forbearance of Mutually Assured Destruction.)

Absent another directive, self-preservation seems to be the prime directive for *all* living things on this earth. It is the nature of life acting within the terrible circumstances of having been born into a world that requires the destruction of another, in order for itself to survive.

Isn't it strange that in order for you to live, something else must die?

It certainly doesn't appear to be the motif of an all-loving Creator. The prime directive is blind, brutal, and guarantees painful destruction. Some would argue that it makes life stronger. But after several *millions* of years of "dog eat dog," the dinosaurs never appeared to gain any knowledge beyond that of getting food and keeping from being food.

Yes, they certainly got stronger and better, but only at staying at the same place.

Humans, on the other hand, after only a few hundred thousand years, are exploring the galaxy with spacecraft. We're creating vaccines to combat disease, solving complex mathematical problems, speaking directly to each other with audio and video from thousands of miles apart, and creating machines with intelligence potentially greater than our own! In the slimmest period of time, we are light years ahead of the dinosaurs.

What's the difference between us and the dinosaurs?

It is this: the *'every man for himself'* selfishness of dog-eat-dog has *proven* to be an inferior form of survival than when we share our intelligence for the benefit of all. 'Every man for himself' is the *least* efficient form of survival. It is the most instinctual, but the least efficient.

We'd still be in the Stone Age had we not shared our discoveries and intelligence with each other.

We learn from each other. In that way, the best ideas tend to improve all of our lives, while the bad ideas that don't work fall by the wayside. *Everyone gets the benefit of the best.* It's shared progress.

Through shared progress, we don't have to keep relearning the same things over and over. Progress and the benefit of knowledge becomes much more efficient.

But given today's technological *destructive* power, division against each other all but guarantees the destruction of humankind. The rate of technological advancement and greed is quickly outpacing our moral aptitude.

Racism, nationalism, authoritarianism, social acceptance of outright lies, dishonest "news" and social platforms, that breed division and hatred based on all of the above, are on the rise. It's a powder keg, waiting to destroy us all. All it takes is for a narcissistic self-serving sociopath to want to rule the world. And there appears to be no shortage of them.

The Doomsday Clock to human destruction has been kept by the Bulletin of the Atomic Scientists for 75 years. Go here:

[https://thebulletin.org/doomsday-clock/]

Here is its opening statement:

2021 Doomsday Clock Announcement

January 27, 2021

> "Human beings can manage the dangers posed by modern technology, even in times of crisis. But if humanity is to avoid an existential catastrophe—one that would dwarf anything it has yet seen—national leaders must do a far better job of countering disinformation, heeding science, and cooperating to diminish global risks."

Right now, the greed of self and tribal preservation is killing not just ourselves but the Mother Earth on which we live. We are acting as a cancer to this earth, without regard to the destruction of the very host that gives us life.

But the common enemy of all life goes far beyond our selves. It is Nature, itself. Nature is blind, and cares nothing for any form of life whatsoever. It can't. It's just a mechanical machine, a set of imperatives that functions in relation to its interactions with itself, aka, physics. The good news is that …

There are at least two ways to overcome Nature, *and* our own self destruction:

1. through knowledge, (external), i.e., science; and,

2. through action, (internal), i.e., spirituality

Spirituality is the overcoming of nature through empathy. It is *extending our senses* beyond the needs and confines of our personal organism, to the rest of the world. It's an attempt to *resonate* with all else.

Imagine how excellent this world would be for the human experience, and for the world itself, if empathy & knowledge were the common method of survival, instead of the self-preservation default mode of violence?

Combining science with spirituality is the winning ticket. *Not* the superstition of religion, mind you, which is anti-science. I'm talking about the real McCoy, the kind of spirituality defined as The Spiritual Law - to love thy neighbor as thyself. The simplicity of this is mind-boggling.

No one needs religion to be spiritual. Spirituality is a state of mind, not an affiliation with a social group. This isn't to say that spiritual social groups are bad. It's just that they are functionally separate things; one is not the other.

Of course, it takes an environment where others are in agreement with this simple law, or it quickly reverts to barbarity. Historically, the agreement process is known as "civilization."

With civilization, certain types of actions are deemed unfavorable for a civil society. And from that civility, certain forms of morality become codified. And those become the "norms" or "laws" of the land, or group.

For example, murder is typically deemed "wrong," uncivil; or in the case of law, "illegal," because generally *we don't want to be murdered*. The Golden Rule, a maxim, to treat others as you would like to be treated, goes back to Confucian times, around 551-479 BCE.

But the idea of the maxim as a form of law, perhaps the oldest form of civil law in written history, can be found in the Code of Hammurabi, circa 1755-1750 BC, Babylon. In short, this stuff ain't exactly new. These ideas have been around since ... civilization.

It's an agreement on how to treat each other, so that we can *all* survive better.

Of course, lower forms of creatures, (we refer to humans of this uncivil mindset as reptiles), could no more subscribe to this form of existence than the spider trying to be a farmer. It's driven by its nature without recourse. And as best we can tell, so were the dinosaurs, which might explain why they never got past themselves.

Some of us, on the other hand, possess something far greater: the ability to deny our destructive instincts and imagine a better future, and to *act in a way* that builds that future. Heaven on earth is a promise that only we can make; to ourselves.

But to do so, we *must* overcome the natural instinct to care only about ourselves and our tribe. Admittedly, it's not easy. But it must be done. **We must increase our capacity for civilization.**

The method is a simple one-step process. It is enshrined in the Spiritual Law.

To "love thy neighbor as thyself" has ever been the message of true religion, the subject of all spiritual discourse, and the means of tuning the individual and collective soul to the divine. **The Spiritual Law paves the way for advanced civilization.**

Advanced civilization is the only way advanced life can wield advanced knowledge. Absent *advanced* civilization, advanced knowledge becomes little more than an advanced tool for destruction and barbarity. Nukes, for example, come to mind.

The inevitable consequence is, back to square one, dog eat dog. Or, back to square zero, total extinction. Either way, the failsafe against advanced knowledge, *without* advanced civilization, is its own destruction. The only difference between the two is the extent.

Where are we in this saga of civilization? According to the Bulletin of the Atomic Scientists, the Doomsday Clock to human destruction is now at 100 seconds to midnight. 'Closer than we've ever been.

All paths to destruction seem to be imminent, save one. This is the Spiritual Challenge. And it appears to be the most difficult.

We either overcome *wrong decisions* to value ourselves into tribes of, [put infinite number of social divisions here], or we take responsibility for *correct decisions* aimed at advanced civility, regardless of our social distinctions.

"Love thy neighbor as thyself" encompasses each means of overcoming nature. Love extends beyond the senses. And it affords the best possible outcomes from actions.

For some, it is the most difficult form of action; but for all, it is the most rewarding. It holds true on the inner spiritual planes, as well as the outer, material one.

Your challenge is to …

Pick a side.

Put on the dog-tags of the *'every man for himself'* selfishness of dog eat dog. Or, put on the glistening nimbus of divinity and *become* the avatar of your highest being.

In the first choice, destruction of humankind is the inevitable conclusion; (thank you for your service).

In the second choice, whether there is a heaven or not, you've made *this* world, in *this* life, a better place than how you found it. Let the chips fall where they may, in any other.

And with that, I bid you with a tip of the hat, adieu.

Yours Truly,

Dorian.

6

MUSIC FOR INNER TRAVEL

*E*xample Playlists

The Relaxation/Calming/Sleep genres are often mixed, as if they are the same. Pull up one and you'll get a bit of either. The recommendations listed below are meant to clarify by function for inner & spiritual travel.

The titles chosen below are among my favorites based upon their ability to do its job, i.e., sleep & pre-sleep, and inner travel.

Your tastes will eventually be customized specifically for you, as you listen to more from each genre and assign them to the right category.

A Few Notes About What You're Doing with This Stuff

First, only bother to do this type of listening when you're uninterrupted and preferably with headphones or earbuds using high, or very high-quality audio settings.

Second, **turn the music down!** Start listening with the volume low enough to barely hear it. As it gets quieter, or as you transition into a relaxed state, the music will seem louder. If necessary, turn it down a bit more.

Note: the higher the quality your equipment and settings, the lower the volume needs to be. Loud music may permanently destroy your ear drums; you need to respect this right from the start.

Adjusting Audio Quality

You can set these Settings within the app. (In Pandora go to **Content Settings**, in Spotify go to **Preferences** > Settings > Audio Quality.) Note: you can get the highest Audio Quality music via **Download**, instead of through streaming, but the higher quality uses more storage. Of course, **Normalize** volume for all audios.

Still your thoughts and treat the session as meditation. (For years, I've treated music of this kind as my own private slice of heaven. Get to bed early and you'll see what I mean.)

For Sleep & Pre-Sleep Music

Listen more to the tonal undercurrents that captures your attention as a physical sensation.

If the sensation is pleasurable or elicits fond memories, follow it and allow it to show you what's there.

If it elicits new memories, say, of future places that you've yet to visit but offers a good sensation, follow it and allow it to show you what's there.

At this point, you're not looking for sleep, yet, but for a sensation that separates your typical awake awareness into the inner awareness of complete alertness while your body enters a state of stilled quietness.

If you drift off to sleep, no harm, no foul. Try to notice the transition phase between the two states. It's that in-between transition state that you're really looking for anyways. The quicker you can get to that state without losing lucidity, the quicker the transition into inner travel. And that's the goal.

That's the function of this type of music as it relates to conscious travel away from the physical world.

There are many artists and producers of the Relaxing / Sleep Pre-Sleep Music genre. I have more than 100 artists in my playlists. At the top of this list is **Liquid Mind**.

For several years and over many albums **Liquid Mind** have produced the perfect type of sound for pre-sleep, (and often inner travel, too), while still sounding like music. They have it down.

I originally had links pointing to each song title, but the links are unruly, and I decided to leave them out, especially since they are prone to change. Most titles can be found on either Spotify or Pandora applications; but you'll have to create the playlists yourself, sorry.

Type 1: Sleep & Pre-Sleep Music

Use this type of music for pre-sleep or for drifting off to sleep with a mind on finding the undertones to latch onto for inner traveling.

Artist: **Liquid Mind** (https://liquidmindmusic.com/):

Laguna Indigo (Parts 1, 2, & 3) - Liquid Mind III: Balance

Into the Light - Pt. 1 - Liquid Mind IX: Lullaby

Mountain Lullaby - Liquid Mind IX: Lullaby

Breath in Me - Liquid Mind VIII: Sleep

Reflection - Liquid Mind, Liquid Mind VII: Reflection

Velvet Morning - Liquid Mind VI: Spirit

Etc.

Artist: **Llewellyn**

Sleep Gentle Sleep - Llewellyn - Sleep Gold (1:01:26)

Reiki Gold – Llewellyn, Reiki Gold

The Healing Waterfall - Llewellyn - Reiki Gold

The Journeys End - Aura Cleansing & Grounding - Llewellyn - Reiki Gold

Artist: **Aeoliah**

Innocence & Purity of the Heart – Aeoliah's Sample Elixir, Music Anthology 3

Artist: **Yuri Sazonoff**

The Soothing Source – performer: Dan Gibson's Solitudes – album: European Spa

Artist: **2002**

Sunlight Through A Feather – album: Wings II Return to Freedom

Oasis - album: Believe

Breathing Light – album: Wings II Return to Freedom

Artist: **Kamal**

Healing - Kamal, Quiet Earth

Artists: **Craig Padilla, Zero Ohms & Skip Murphy**

Perspective of Disappearance – album: Beyond the Portal

Artist: **Rudy Adrian**

Under Orion - Rudy Adrian, MoonWater

Artist: **Blank & Jones**

Souvenir – Blank & Jones – Relax Edition 6

Type 2: Resonant Drifting / Inner Travel

Use this type of music when you already know what you're looking for and don't need the music. Once you've stilled your mind and shut down your internal dialog, these sounds can take you into new worlds quickly.

Artist: **Phillip Wilkerson**

Sweet Eva Lena - Phillip Wilkerson – album: Highlands (2012)

Artist: **Resonant Drift**

Beyond the Vision - Resonant Drift, Passages

Transformation - Resonant Drift, Passages

Artist: **Drifting in Silence**

Infall - Drifting In Silence – album: Truth

Artist: **Steve Roach**

Where Rasa Lives - Steve Roach - album: Back to Life

Artist: **SubtractiveLAD**

Pebbles And Shells – SubtractiveLAD – album: Where The Land Meets The Sky

7

BACK MATTER & REFERENCES

Definition Of Terms

Inner - "the *Inner*" refers to the essence of a person, the soul, the consciousness that makes you, *you*. It is that which distinguishes your "being" from your body.

Outer – "the Outer" refers to the physical, (objective), external world.

Privacy Policy

The short version: I respect your privacy and hate spam.

The long version:

https://spiritualvectors.com/privacy-policy/

Links

Web based links are subject to change without notice and may lead to discontinued web pages and 404 Error pages, etc. The author has no control over this but may update linked pages in future revisions as necessary.

Important Disclaimers

Time is of the essence.

Products & Services Policy

Products/services mentioned, individually or web based, are based on the sole opinion of the author's experience and no warranty of fitness or safety of said products are to be assumed or implied. Neither the author nor publisher or associates shall be held liable for the use or misuse of any product or service, or anything else mentioned in this book. The information presented is for entertainment and reference purposes only.